EGYPT

Tom Streissguth

Lerner Books • London • New York • Minneapolis

First published in the United Kingdom in 2009 by
Lerner Books,
Dalton House,
60 Windsor Avenue,
London SW19 2RR

Website address: www.lernerbooks.co.uk

This edition was updated and edited for UK publication by Discovery Books Ltd.,
First Floor, 2 College Street, Ludlow, Shropshire SY8 1AN

British Library Cataloguing in Publication Data

Streissguth, Thomas, 1958-
Egypt. - 2nd ed. - (Country explorers)
1. Egypt - Juvenile literature
I. Title
962'.055

ISBN-13: 978 0 7613 4282 3

Printed in Singapore

Table of Contents

TUNISIA

MEDITERRANEAN SEA

ALGERIA

LIBYA

Welcome!

We're heading to Egypt! Egypt lies on the continent of Africa. The River Nile runs through Egypt. The Nile is the longest river in the world.

Egypt touches the countries of Sudan in the south and Libya in the west. The Red Sea lies to the east and the Mediterranean Sea is north of Egypt. The Sinai Peninsula attaches Egypt to the continent of Asia.

Egypt

Tourists often visit Egyptian beaches on the Red Sea.

NIGER

4

CHAD

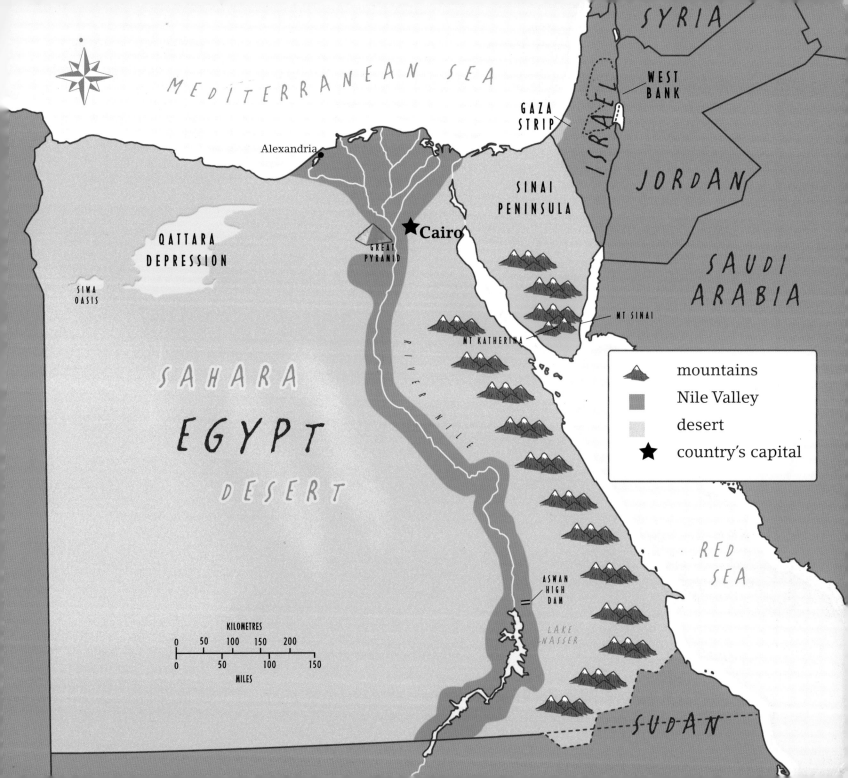

The River Nile

Would you like to sail down the Nile? Then jump on board a felucca! A felucca is an Egyptian sailing boat. On a felucca, you can travel from southern Egypt to the Mediterranean Sea.

Feluccas sail on the Nile as it flows through the city of Aswan.

Towards the end of the trip, you will pass through Cairo. North of Cairo, the Nile branches into smaller rivers. They flow into the Mediterranean. The rivers form a triangle. This area is called a delta.

EGYPT

The Nile Delta seen from space

Dear Gran,

Yesterday I sailed in a felucca on the Nile! It was a windy day, so the sailing boat went very fast. I saw lots of green fields on the riverbanks. Just past them, high red cliffs showed where the desert starts. Cool!

See you soon,

Bobby

Gran
Your To
Anywhe
UK

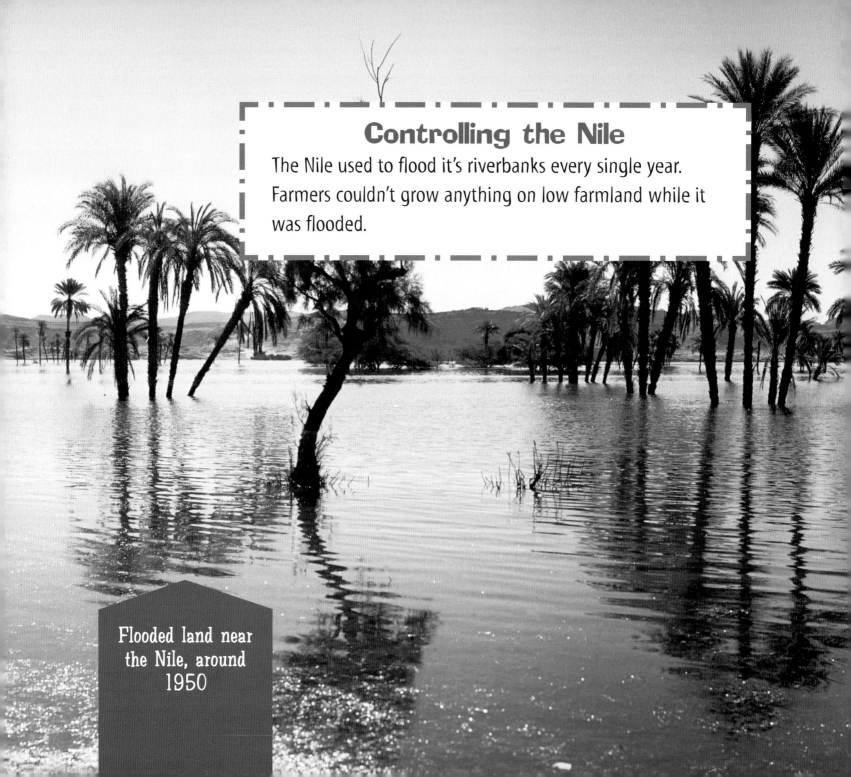

Controlling the Nile

The Nile used to flood it's riverbanks every single year. Farmers couldn't grow anything on low farmland while it was flooded.

Flooded land near the Nile, around 1950

In 1970, the Aswan High Dam was completed. It holds back water from the Nile. It keeps the river from flooding. This lets farmers grow more crops on their land.

The Aswan High Dam

The Sahara

Egyptians do not need raincoats to keep dry! That is because the Sahara covers most of the country. The Sahara is a huge desert. Rain hardly ever falls there. Sandy plains stretch across much of the Sahara. Some parts of the desert have mountains.

Desert winds form sand dunes in many parts of the Sahara.

Not many people live in the desert. However, some people settle on oases. Oases are places in the desert where there is water. Crops and trees can grow in these places.

Thousands of people live at the Siwa Oasis.

Country Life

Many Egyptians live on small farms near the Nile. Egyptian farmers are called fellahin. Some fellahin farm cotton, rice and wheat. Others grow vegetables such as maize.

Donkeys help farmers by carrying heavy loads.

Map Whiz Quiz

Trace the outline of Egypt on pages 4 and 5 onto a sheet of paper. Find the body of water to the right of Egypt. That is the Red Sea. Colour it red. Mark it with an *E* for east. Find the Mediterranean Sea. Colour it blue. Mark it with an *N* for north. Find the River Nile. Colour it green, since green plants can grow near it.

Fellahin also tend date palm trees. These trees produce dates, a kind of fruit.

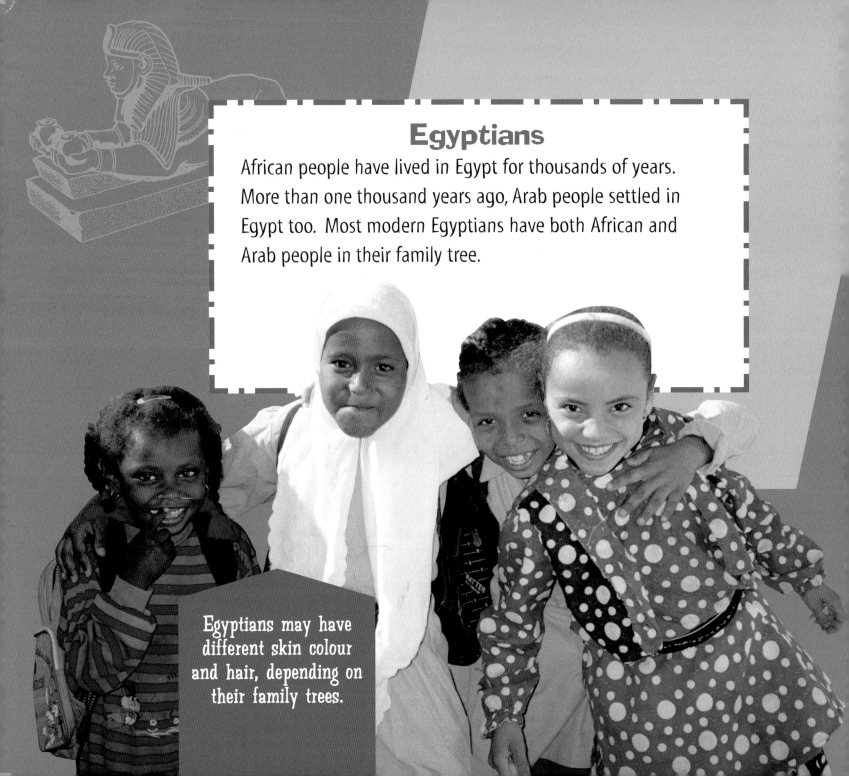

Egyptians

African people have lived in Egypt for thousands of years. More than one thousand years ago, Arab people settled in Egypt too. Most modern Egyptians have both African and Arab people in their family tree.

Egyptians may have different skin colour and hair, depending on their family trees.

People called Nubians used to live along the Nile in southern Egypt. Many Nubians moved to northern cities. Other Egyptians are desert nomads. Nomads travel from place to place instead of living in one spot.

Nomads

Some Egyptians are nomads. They travel across the Sahara for most of the year. One group of nomads is the Bedouin. They live in tents and herd sheep, goats and camels. Some modern Bedouin have become farmers. The government provides schools and medical care for Bedouin farmers.

A Bedouin couple

This Egyptian family takes a ride on camels.

Family

How many brothers and sisters do you have? In Egypt, parents like to have big families. Most children have three, four, or even five brothers and sisters.

Egyptian families stay together. Many married couples live with the husband's parents. The husband's brothers, their families and his sisters might squeeze in too. The house can get really crowded, but Egyptians don't mind. They love to have their families nearby.

A large family visits the pyramids.

Big City

Cairo is the largest city in Egypt. It's also the country's capital. Cairo has modern skyscrapers, motorways and colourful signs. It also has traditional shops and cafés.

The River Nile flows through central Cairo.

Cairo's busy streets can be very loud and jammed with traffic.

Cairo's streets are very busy. Cars pass people riding donkeys. Horses pull carts past children playing football. Some people push carts loaded with goods to sell. The carts are shops on wheels.

Homes

Some people live above shops in Egypt's cities. Others live in tall blocks of flats. In the country, Egyptians build houses from mud bricks. Most houses have two rooms. People gather and eat in one room and sleep in the other.

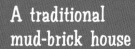
A traditional mud-brick house

Some Egyptian houses have a courtyard in the middle. People might cook their meals in courtyards. They also keep their animals in the courtyard at night to keep them safe.

Some houses are painted with brightly coloured murals.

Arabic

Egyptians speak Arabic. Egyptian children learn how to read and write Arabic when they are in school. People write and read Arabic from right to left.

Picture Writing

In ancient times, Egyptians used pictures to write. These pictures are called hieroglyphs. The symbols decorate the walls of tombs and other ancient buildings.

Religion

Most Egyptians are Muslims. Muslims follow the religion of Islam. They often go to pray at mosques. A mosque is an Islamic house of prayer. Egypt's cities and villages have many mosques.

Inside the Al-Azhar Mosque, one of Cairo's oldest mosques

Most mosques have a minaret. A minaret is a tall, thin tower. A man called a muezzin climbs the minaret five times a day. He calls out a chant from the top. The chant reminds Muslims that it is time to pray.

This mosque and minaret are in the city of Alexandria on the Mediterranean Sea.

Festivals!

Egyptians celebrate springtime with a festival called *Sham Al Nessim*, which means 'scent of the breeze'. During this festival, Egyptian families enjoy picnics at gardens or at parks.

In Cairo, Egyptians swim and row boats on the Nile during Sham Al Nessim.

Ramadan

Ramadan is the holy month of the Islamic calendar. Muslims fast during the days of Ramadan. They don't eat or drink anything from sunrise until sunset. They eat a meal called *iftar* when the sun sets. Friends and families often eat together. Many people follow the rules of Islam more closely during Ramadan.

At the end of Ramadan, Egyptians celebrate Eid ul-Fitr. They gather with their families and have a large feast.

Mawlid al-Nabi marks the birthday of Muhammad. Muhammad started Islam. On Mawlid al-Nabi, big tents fill the streets. Egyptians bang drums and shake tambourines inside the tents. Some people dance and sing. At night, a parade winds through the town.

Muslims share the iftar meal at sunset during Ramadan.

27

Students study the Quran in a village school with no desks or chairs.

Learning

At the age of six, Egyptian children start primary school. When they reach the age of twelve, they begin secondary school. Lots of children go to work after they are fourteen years old. Others move on to college or university.

Egyptian schools are crowded! Egyptian students often have to share their books, desks and seats. The government has built many new schools to help change this.

Girls share desks at a school in Cairo. Many Egyptian schools have separate classrooms for girls and boys.

Shopping

Shoppers in most Egyptian towns go to the souk. A souk is a marketplace. People can buy and sell many types of goods there. One lane of the souk is lined with rug shops. Another offers saucepans. Spices are for sale nearby.

Egyptians shop at an outdoor market in Cairo.

There are no price tags at a souk. A buyer and a seller bargain over the price of an item. They try to find a price they can both agree on.

Camel Buying

If you plan to cross the Sahara, head to the camel market in Cairo! Camels are very useful animals to the Egyptians. Can you guess why? Camels hardly ever need a drink of water. They can cross the desert carrying a heavy load or a rider. In cities, camels also help Egyptian families make money. Tourists often pay an Egyptian man to take them for a ride on his camel.

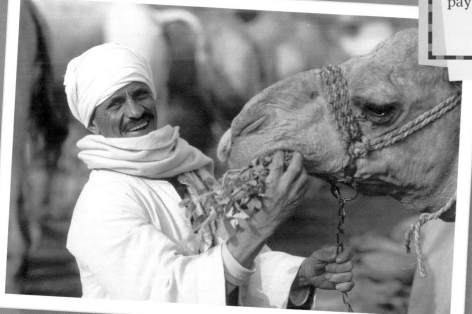

Clothes

Many Egyptians like to wear loose, traditional outfits to keep cool. Men often wear long, loose shirts. They wear small cloth hats called skullcaps to protect their heads from the sun. Women wear long dresses and veils.

Men may wear skullcaps (*above*) or turbans (*right*) on their heads.

Some Egyptians wear European-style clothes. Businesspeople wear suits or dresses to work. Young people often wear a mix of traditional and modern clothing.

Hosni Mubarak, the president of Egypt, and his wife, Suzanne, wear business-style clothing.

Lunchtime

Lunch is the biggest meal of the day in Egypt. Cooks grill chunks of lamb with tomatoes, onions, peppers and spices. Egyptians often cook with tahini — a paste of ground sesame seeds. Baba ghanoush is a mixture of tahini and aubergine. People often eat it with pitta bread.

This Egyptian meal includes sweet potato salad; baba ghanoush; a salad of tomato, cucumber and parsley with lemon juice; pitta bread and fried fish with tomatoes.

Egyptians like to end their lunch with fruit.
Still hungry? Egyptians love to snack on
sweet, sticky treats made with honey.

Pitta bread is
cooked in big clay
ovens.

A statue called the Great Sphinx of Giza sits in front of the Pyramid of Khafre.

The Pyramids

In ancient times, kings called pharaohs ruled Egypt. The pharaohs built giant, pyramid-shaped buildings of stone. A king would be buried inside when he died.

When a pharaoh died, ancient Egyptian priests wrapped the body in cloth and placed it in a special coffin. Then the body was put in a secret grave or in a pyramid. Scientists and explorers have found the mummies of some pharaohs.

The Great Pyramid *(front)* and other pyramids are in Giza, a city near Cairo.

Thousands of years ago, a pharaoh named Khufu built the Great Pyramid. When Khufu died, valuable treasures were placed in the pyramid, along with his body. Visitors can see the empty room where the treasure once was.

School's Out!

Egyptian children love to play football. After school, they play in the streets or on school teams. They also like *seega*. Seega is a little bit like noughts and crosses.

Boys play football at the Siwa Oasis.

Egyptian children work with their families too. Many do after-school jobs on farms or look after their younger brothers and sisters. Other children help their parents catch fish or sell goods in markets.

These children are selling tomatoes.

Films and Television

Lights! Camera! Action! More films are made in Egypt than in any other African country. Romance, comedy and action films are popular.

People wait near a poster for an Egyptian film.

40

Egypt produces TV programmes too. Egyptian game shows, comedies and dramas are shown in other Arab countries.

The wives of the presidents of America and Egypt, Laura Bush (*left*) and Suzanne Mubarak visit the set of the Egyptian *Sesame Street*.

Music

Egyptians like lots of different types of music. Farmers and boaters on the Nile sing folk songs. Street musicians might play the flute or the *rebab*. The rebab is like a violin.

The Egyptian band Wust el Balad plays a mix of jazz, blues, Latin and Arabic music.

Egyptian dance music is popular in Egypt and nearby countries. Some Egyptians prefer American rock music or European opera tunes.

Hakim, one of Egypt's biggest pop stars

THE FLAG OF EGYPT

Egypt's flag has a red stripe on top, a white stripe in the middle and a black stripe at the bottom. The red stands for Egypt's struggle for independence. The white stands for the Egyptian Revolution of 1952, when Egyptians took over their government. They put a president in charge instead of a king. The black stripe stands for the end of the hard times that Egyptians suffered under kings and queens. A golden eagle sits in the centre of the flag. The eagle's feet hold a scroll with the country's name written in Arabic.

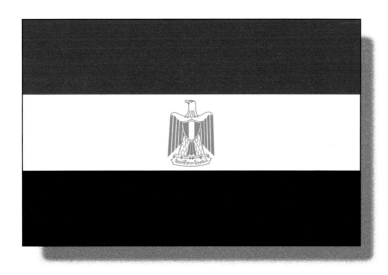

FAST FACTS

FULL COUNTRY NAME: Arab Republic of Egypt

AREA: 1,001,000 square kilometres (387,000 square miles), roughly five times the size of the UK

CAPITAL CITY: Cairo

OFFICIAL LANGUAGE: Arabic

POPULATION: about 80,000,000

SOME MAJOR LANDFORMS:

PENINSULAS: Sinai Peninsula

MOUNTAINS: Sinai and Katherina

DESERTS: Sahara desert

BASINS: Qattara Depression

RIVERS: River Nile

ANIMALS AND THEIR HABITATS:

DESERT: camels, cobras, horned vipers, scorpions

RIVERS: crocodiles

MUDFLATS: flamingoes

OCEAN: tiger sharks

GRASSLANDS: hyenas

GLOSSARY

continent: any one of seven large areas of land. The continents are Africa, Antarctica, Asia, Australia, Europe, North America and South America.

courtyard: an open area surrounded by walls. Similar to a back garden.

delta: a triangle-shaped area of land where a river enters the sea. The river leaves behind mud or sand on the delta.

desert: a dry, sandy region

desert basin: a sunken area of a desert

hieroglyphs: pictures and symbols that ancient Egyptians used in writing

mummies: dead bodies that ancient Egyptians wrapped in cloth to preserve them for a long time

Muslim: a person who practises the religion of Islam

nomad: a person who wanders from place to place instead of living in one spot

oases: places in the desert where there is water. Trees and crops can grow on an oasis.

peninsula: an area of land with water on three sides

pharaohs: kings of ancient Egypt

pyramid: a stone building with four triangle-shaped sides, built by ancient Egyptians

TO LEARN MORE

BOOKS

Roxbee Cox, Phil. *Who Built the Pyramids?* Usborne Publishing Limited, 2003.

Sands, Emily. *Egyptology: Search for the Temple of Osiris* Templar Publishing, 2005.

Steer, David. *The Wonders of Egypt: A Course in Egyptology* Templar Publishing, 2005.

Turnbull, Stephanie. *Egyptians* Usborne Publishing Limited, 2006.

Tyldesley, Joyce. *Stories from Ancient Egypt: Egyptian Myths and Legends for Children* Rutherford Press Limited, 2005.

WEBSITES

Ancient Egypt
http://www.ancientegypt.co.uk/menu.html
This interactive website, built by the British Museum, lets you explore ancient Egypt, including daily life, pharaohs, mummies and writing. It features stories, lots of photos and challenges.

History for Kids — Egypt
http://www.historyforkids.org/learn/egypt/

Visit this website to learn the facts about different parts of Egyptian life; from the clothes they wear, to what they like to eat, to the types of buildings they construct.

INDEX

The photographs in this book are used with the permission of: © Gerard Hancock/Art Directors, p 4; © Michele Burgess, pp 6, 16, 18; NASA, p 7; © Paul Almasy/CORBIS, p 8; © Jon Arnold Images/Alamy, p 9; © age fotostock/SuperStock, pp 10, 21, 24, 31, 34; © Kurt Scholz/SuperStock, p 11; AP Photo/Ben Curtis, p 12; © Kevin Fleming/CORBIS, p 13; © Cory Langley, pp 14, 20; © SuperStock, Inc./SuperStock, p 15; © Nik Wheeler/CORBIS, p 17; © P L Mitchell/Art Directors, p 19; © saturno dona'/Alamy, p 22; © Gregor Schuster/zefa/Corbis, p 23; © Bettmann/CORBIS, p 25; AP Photo/Amr Nabil, p 26; © Khaled Desouki/AFP/Getty Images, p 27; © Jean Dominique DALLET/Alamy, p 28; AP Photo/Mohamed El-Dakhakhny, p 29; © David Harding/Art Directors, p 30; © Thomas Hartwell/CORBIS, p 32 (left); © Adina Tovy/Art Directors, p 32 (right); AP Photo/Jalil Bounhar, p 33; © Michele Burgess/SuperStock, p 35; © David Sutherland/Photographer's Choice/Getty Images, p 36; © Scott Olson/Getty Images, p 37 (left); © Martin Gray/National Geographic/Getty Images, p 37 (right); © Sylvain Grandadam/The Image Bank/Getty Images, p 38; © John R Kreul/Independent Picture Service, p 39; AP Photo/Talal Amr, p 40; © AFP/Getty Images, p 41; AP Photo/Mohamed al Sehety, p 42; AP Photo/John McConnico, p 43 Illustrations by © Bill Hauser/Independent Picture Service.

Cover: © Jose Fuste Raga/CORBIS